MY JOURNAL

A Giroux Recipe
MY JOURNAL

Published by BooxAi
ISBN: 978-965-577-991-2

MY JOURNAL

For My Thoughts

A GIROUX RECIPE

Contents

Welcome to MY JOURNAL! This is your journal to write and document your own ideas, thoughts and feelings. It is a safe place to express yourself and go over (examine/analyze) your thoughts and issues that come up as you grow.

This journal is planned out to support you at focusing on your own inner beliefs and values to help guide your path forward into living the best authentic life that's unique to you!

Fill out your journal daily. Maybe keep it beside your bed, so you remember to fill it out every day. Don't worry if you forget to fill it out one of the days, just pick up where you left off. Soon it will become like another daily thing to do, just like brushing your teeth.

However you would like to fill out your journal is totally up to you. You can use colorful pens or plain pencils, add stickers etc. - its your journal to be creative as you like!

You can fill it out by yourself or do it for fun with your parents/a family member or a friend.

On every 8th day there is an EVALUATE day to look back over the last 7 days and summarize your week.

There are some blank pages in the journal for you to create your own drawings, poems, quotes, thoughts or doodles. Feel free to write what-ever you like in it - this is your journal, just for you!

We hope you enjoy using this journal and hopefully, it creates a lifelong habit of documenting great challenges and wonderful moments in your life to help you make sense of yourself and the world around you.

With happiest thoughts.

This journal was created for children from 6 to 12 years old, so depending on the age/stage of your child some of the questions maybe a bit advanced and would be most suitable to be filled In alongside an adult for support and clarification. This journal aims to support our children to learn about themselves and lead their most authentic life and for us to help them celebrate their uniqueness!

Here at THE CENTER PROGRAM we believe that kindness to yourself and others is one of the cornerstone pieces to living a life of true happiness. Kindness quotes, questioning and values are Interwoven throughout and serve as a backbone to all our books.

DAY 1   DATE: _______________________

EXERCISE **I did today:** ___________________ 

I ate today:

I ate today:

How much WATER **did I drink today?**
Circle one

NONE   A LITTLE   ENOUGH   LOTS

Today I FELT:

____

____

HIGHLIGHT OF MY DAY TODAY:

____

____

TODAY I AM GRATEFUL FOR:

(highlight the things you are grateful for and draw some pictures if you like!)

ME

SUNSHINE

RAINBOWS

FRIENDS

BOOKS

ANIMALS

FAMILY

HUGS

FOOD

LOVE

TREES

MY BODY

FRESH AIR

MUSIC

FREEDOM

BIRDS SINGING

BUGS

 DATE: ___________________________

Something KIND I did today:

____

Today I am GRATEFUL for:
1.
2.
3.
4.

My FEELINGS and EMOTIONS today

MORNING   AFTERNOON   EVENING

Something that made me SMILE today:

____

THINGS I LOVE
ABOUT BEING ME!

 DATE: ___________________________

EXERCISE **I did today:** _______________________

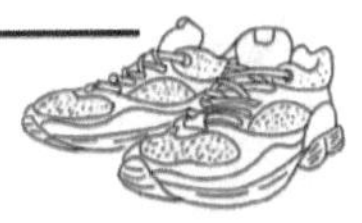

NUTRITIOUS FOOD **I ate today:**

UNHEALTHY FOOD **I ate today:**

How much WATER **did I drink today?**
Circle one

NONE   A LITTLE   ENOUGH   LOTS

Today I FELT:

____

____

HIGHLIGHT OF MY DAY TODAY:

____

____

Things
That
Make ME
Happy!

DATE: _______________________

Something KIND I did today:

____

Today I am GRATEFUL for:
1.
2.
3.
4.

My FEELINGS and EMOTIONS today

MORNING   AFTERNOON   EVENING

Something that made me SMILE today:

____

HAPPINESS
IS ENJOYING THE
LITTLEST THINGS

 DATE: ________________________

EXERCISE **I did today:** ______________________

NUTRITIOUS FOOD **I ate today:**

UNHEALTHY FOOD **I ate today:**

How much WATER **did I drink today?**
Circle one

NONE   A LITTLE   ENOUGH   LOTS

Today I FELT:

____

____

HIGHLIGHT OF MY DAY TODAY:

____

____

 DATE: _______________________________

Something KIND I did today:

____

Today I am GRATEFUL for:
  1.
  2.
  3.
  4.

My FEELINGS and EMOTIONS today

MORNING   AFTERNOON   EVENING

Something that made me SMILE today:

____

My
Favorite
Foods

DAY 7   DATE: _______________________

EXERCISE **I did today:** _______________________

NUTRITIOUS FOOD **I ate today:**

UNHEALTHY FOOD **I ate today:**

How much WATER **did I drink today?**
Circle one

NONE   A LITTLE   ENOUGH   LOTS

Today I FELT:

____
____

HIGHLIGHT OF MY DAY TODAY:

____
____

BE A
pineapple
STAND TALL
wear a crown
AND
be sweet

 DATE: _________________________

EVALUATE

The BEST **thing that happened this week:**

____

____

The WORST **thing that happened this week:**

____

____

What could I do NEXT TIME **to make it different/better?**

____

____

What did I do that was the most KIND **this week?**

____

____

What was I CURIOUS **about this week?**

____

____

What did I CREATE **this week?**

____

____

Save/Spend/Share

How much money do I have? Am I saving for something? How much does it cost?

____

____

____

What could I do this week to earn some extra pocket money?

____

____

____

What am I planning to focus on or ACHIEVE for this next week ahead?

____

____

____

 DATE: _______________________

Something KIND I did today:

____

Today I am GRATEFUL for:
1.
2.
3.
4.

My FEELINGS and EMOTIONS today

MORNING   AFTERNOON   EVENING

Something that made me SMILE today:

____

THINGS
I AM
GOOD AT:

DAY 10   DATE: _______________________

EXERCISE **I did today:** _______________________ 

NUTRITIOUS FOOD **I ate today:**

UNHEALTHY FOOD **I ate today:**

How much WATER **did I drink today?**
Circle one

NONE   A LITTLE   ENOUGH   LOTS

Today I FELT:

____

____

HIGHLIGHT OF MY DAY TODAY:

____

____

Some things I WORRY about:

DAY 11 DATE: _______________________

Something KIND I did today:

____

Today I am GRATEFUL for:
1.
2.
3.
4.

My FEELINGS and EMOTIONS today

MORNING   AFTERNOON   EVENING

Something that made me SMILE today:

____

SMILE OFTEN
THINK POSITIVELY
GIVE THANKS
LAUGH LOUDLY
LOVE OTHERS
AND
DREAM BIG

DAY 12   DATE: ___________________

EXERCISE **I did today:** _________________________

NUTRITIOUS FOOD **I ate today:**

UNHEALTHY FOOD **I ate today:**

How much WATER **did I drink today?**
Circle one

NONE   A LITTLE   ENOUGH   LOTS

Today I FELT:

____

____

HIGHLIGHT OF MY DAY TODAY:

____

____

guilty
anxious
worried
insecure
upset
angry
It's OK to feel the way I feel.
Sometimes we don't like how our emotions make us feel, but remember everybody feels that way sometimes.
jealous
frustrated
envious
sad
scared
ashamed
lonely

DAY 13 DATE: _______________________

Something KIND **I did today:**

____

Today I am GRATEFUL **for:**
   1.
   2.
   3.
   4.

My FEELINGS **and** EMOTIONS **today**

MORNING   AFTERNOON   EVENING

Something that made me SMILE **today:**

____

 DATE: _______________________

EXERCISE **I did today:** _____________________________

 NUTRITIOUS FOOD **I ate today:**

 UNHEALTHY FOOD **I ate today:**

How much WATER **did I drink today?
Circle one**

NONE   A LITTLE   ENOUGH   LOTS

Today I FELT:

____

____

HIGHLIGHT OF MY DAY TODAY:

____

____

3 words I would use to describe
MYSELF:

1

2

3

 DATE: _______________________

Something KIND I **did today:**

____

Today I am GRATEFUL **for:**
1.
2.
3.
4.

My FEELINGS **and** EMOTIONS **today**

MORNING   AFTERNOON   EVENING

Something that made me SMILE **today:**

____

Important things my FAMILY has taught me:

 DATE: ___________________________

EVALUATE

The BEST **thing that happened this week:**

____

____

The WORST **thing that happened this week**:

____

____

What could I do NEXT TIME **to make it different/better?**

____

____

What did I do that was the most KIND **this week?**

____

____

What was I CURIOUS **about this week?**

____

____

What did I CREATE **this week?**

____

____

Save/Spend/Share

How much money do I have? Am I saving for something? How much does it cost?

____

____

____

What could I do this week to earn some extra pocket money?

____

____

____

What am I planning to focus on or ACHIEVE for this next week ahead?

____

____

____

DAY 17   DATE: _______________________

EXERCISE **I did today:** _______________________ 

 ## NUTRITIOUS FOOD **I ate today:**

UNHEALTHY FOOD **I ate today:**

How much WATER **did I drink today?**
Circle one

NONE   A LITTLE   ENOUGH   LOTS

Today I FELT:

____
____

HIGHLIGHT OF MY DAY TODAY:

____
____

Some GOOD MANNERS ARE

Saying HELLO when you see someone

Saying PLEASE when asking for something

Saying THANK YOU when you receive something

Saying SORRY when you have done something wrong

And asking for FORGIVENESS

Say EXCUSE ME if someone is blocking your way

Or if you need to interrupt a conversation

TAKE TURNS to share your toys

And above all BE KIND TO ALL!

DATE: ______________________

Something KIND **I did today:**

____

Today I am GRATEFUL **for:**
1.
2.
3.
4.

My FEELINGS **and** EMOTIONS **today**

MORNING   AFTERNOON   EVENING

Something that made me SMILE **today:**

____

IF YOU WERE A SUPERHERO WHAT SUPERPOWERS
WOULD YOU HAVE?

-
-
-

what would be your SUPERHERO name?

____

Draw your SUPERHERO self here

Tonight before you drift off to sleep imagine yourself as a SuperHero and visualize stories/movies you star in using your superpowers.

DAY 19 DATE: _______________________

EXERCISE **I did today:** _______________________

NUTRITIOUS FOOD **I ate today:**

UNHEALTHY FOOD **I ate today:**

How much WATER **did I drink today?**
Circle one

NONE   A LITTLE   ENOUGH   LOTS

Today I FELT:

____

____

HIGHLIGHT OF MY DAY TODAY:

____

____

DATE: _______________________

Something KIND I did today:

____

Today I am GRATEFUL for:
1.
2.
3.
4.

My FEELINGS and EMOTIONS today

MORNING   AFTERNOON   EVENING

Something that made me SMILE today:

____

It's OK to be a SCAREDY CAT

It means your about to do something

really really

BRAVE!

DAY 21 DATE: ___________________________

EXERCISE **I did today:** _______________________ 

 NUTRITIOUS FOOD **I ate today:**

 UNHEALTHY FOOD **I ate today:**

How much WATER **did I drink today?
Circle one**

NONE   A LITTLE   ENOUGH   LOTS

Today I FELT:

____

____

HIGHLIGHT OF MY DAY TODAY:

____

____

When something is BUGGING me I can say:

"Please stop,
I don't like it when you …"

O
R

- I can walk away
- Take 5 deep breaths
- Tell a trusted Adult
- Journal about it

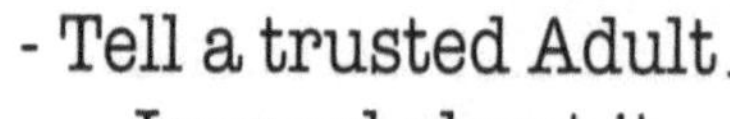

     DATE: _______________________

Something KIND I **did today:**

____

Today I am GRATEFUL **for:**
  1.
  2.
  3.
  4.

My FEELINGS **and** EMOTIONS **today**

MORNING   AFTERNOON   EVENING

Something that made me SMILE **today:**

____

"No act of kindness,
 no matter how small,
 Is ever wasted"

Aesop

 DATE: _______________________

EXERCISE **I did today:** _____________________

 NUTRITIOUS FOOD **I ate today:**

UNHEALTHY FOOD **I ate today:**

How much WATER **did I drink today?**
Circle one

NONE   A LITTLE   ENOUGH   LOTS

Today I FELT:

____

____

HIGHLIGHT OF MY DAY TODAY:

____

____

MY FAVORITE
BOOKS

  DATE: _______________________

EVALUATE

The BEST thing that happened this week:

____

____

The WORST thing that happened this week:

____

____

What could I do NEXT TIME to make it different/better?

____

____

What did I do that was the most KIND this week?

____

____

What was I CURIOUS about this week?

____

____

What did I CREATE this week?

____

____

Save/Spend/Share

How much money do I have? Am I saving for something? How much does it cost?

____

____

____

What could I do this week to earn some extra pocket money?

____

____

____

What am I planning to focus on or ACHIEVE for this next week ahead?

____

____

____

 DATE: _______________________

Something KIND **I did today:**

____

Today I am GRATEFUL **for:**
   1.
   2.
   3.
   4.

My FEELINGS **and** EMOTIONS **today**

MORNING   AFTERNOON   EVENING

Something that made me SMILE **today:**

____

A PET I WOULD LOVE TO HAVE:

 DATE: _______________________

EXERCISE **I did today:** _______________________

 NUTRITIOUS FOOD **I ate today:**

UNHEALTHY FOOD **I ate today:**

How much WATER **did I drink today?**
Circle one

NONE   A LITTLE   ENOUGH   LOTS

Today I FELT:

____

____

HIGHLIGHT OF MY DAY TODAY:

____

____

DATE: _______________________

Something KIND I did today:

____

Today I am GRATEFUL for:
1.
2.
3.
4.

My FEELINGS and EMOTIONS today

MORNING   AFTERNOON   EVENING

Something that made me SMILE today:

____

IF I BELIEVE IT

Then I Can ACHIEVE IT!

 DATE: ___________________________

EXERCISE **I did today:** _______________________

 NUTRITIOUS FOOD **I ate today:**

 UNHEALTHY FOOD **I ate today:**

How much WATER **did I drink today?**
Circle one

NONE   A LITTLE   ENOUGH   LOTS

Today I FELT:

____

____

HIGHLIGHT OF MY DAY TODAY:

____

____

If I could be

INVISIBLE

for a day,

I would:

Something KIND I did today:

____

Today I am GRATEFUL for:
  1.
  2.
  3.
  4.

My FEELINGS and EMOTIONS today

MORNING   AFTERNOON   EVENING

Something that made me SMILE today:

____

"To love and be loved is to feel the sun from both sides."

David Viscott

DAY 30   DATE: _______________________

EXERCISE **I did today:** _____________________ 

NUTRITIOUS FOOD **I ate today:**

UNHEALTHY FOOD **I ate today:**

How much WATER **did I drink today?**
Circle one

NONE   A LITTLE   ENOUGH   LOTS

Today I FELT:

____

____

HIGHLIGHT OF MY DAY TODAY:

____

____

What's the BRAVEST thing I have ever done:

DATE: _______________________

Something KIND I did today:

____

Today I am GRATEFUL for:
1.
2.
3.
4.

My FEELINGS and EMOTIONS today

MORNING   AFTERNOON   EVENING

Something that made me SMILE today:

____

PEOPLE I LOVE:

EVALUATE

The BEST thing that happened this week:

____

____

The WORST thing that happened this week:

____

____

What could I do NEXT TIME to make it different/better?

____

____

What did I do that was the most KIND this week?

____

____

What was I CURIOUS about this week?

____

____

What did I CREATE this week?

____

____

SAVE/SPEND/SHARE

How much money do I have? Am I saving for something? How much does it cost?

____

____

____

What could I do this week to earn some extra pocket money?

____

____

____

What am I planning to focus on or ACHIEVE for this next week ahead?

____

____

____

 DATE: _______________________

EXERCISE **I did today:** _________________ 

NUTRITIOUS FOOD **I ate today:**

UNHEALTHY FOOD **I ate today:**

How much WATER **did I drink today?**
Circle one

NONE   A LITTLE   ENOUGH   LOTS

Today I FELT:

____

____

HIGHLIGHT OF MY DAY TODAY:

____

____

SAY THESE AFFIRMATIONS IN THE MIRROR TO MAKE YOU FEEL GREAT AND BELIEVE IN YOURSELF!

I am loved

I am brave

I am kind

I am a good friend

I am courageous

I believe in myself

I make good choices

I am proud of myself

I try my best

I am a great listener

I am creative

I am capable and can do hard things

I am a great kid

DATE: _______________________

Something KIND I did today:

____

Today I am GRATEFUL for:
1.
2.
3.
4.

My FEELINGS and EMOTIONS today

MORNING   AFTERNOON   EVENING

Something that made me SMILE today:

____

<table><tr><td>**DAY 35**</td><td>DATE: _________________________</td></tr></table>

EXERCISE **I did today:** _______________________

 NUTRITIOUS FOOD **I ate today:**

UNHEALTHY FOOD **I ate today:**

How much WATER **did I drink today?**
Circle one

NONE   A LITTLE   ENOUGH   LOTS

Today I FELT:

____

____

HIGHLIGHT OF MY DAY TODAY:

____

____

Things that make me FRUSTRATED:

1.

2.

3.

Things that make me HAPPY:

1.

2.

3.

DATE: _______________________

Something KIND I did today:

____

Today I am GRATEFUL for:
1.
2.
3.
4.

My FEELINGS and EMOTIONS today

MORNING   AFTERNOON   EVENING

Something that made me SMILE today:

____

My FAVORITE Dinner:

DATE: _______________________

EXERCISE **I did today:** _______________________ 

NUTRITIOUS FOOD **I ate today:**

UNHEALTHY FOOD **I ate today:**

How much WATER **did I drink today?**
Circle one

NONE   A LITTLE   ENOUGH   LOTS

Today I FELT:

____

____

HIGHLIGHT OF MY DAY TODAY:

____

____

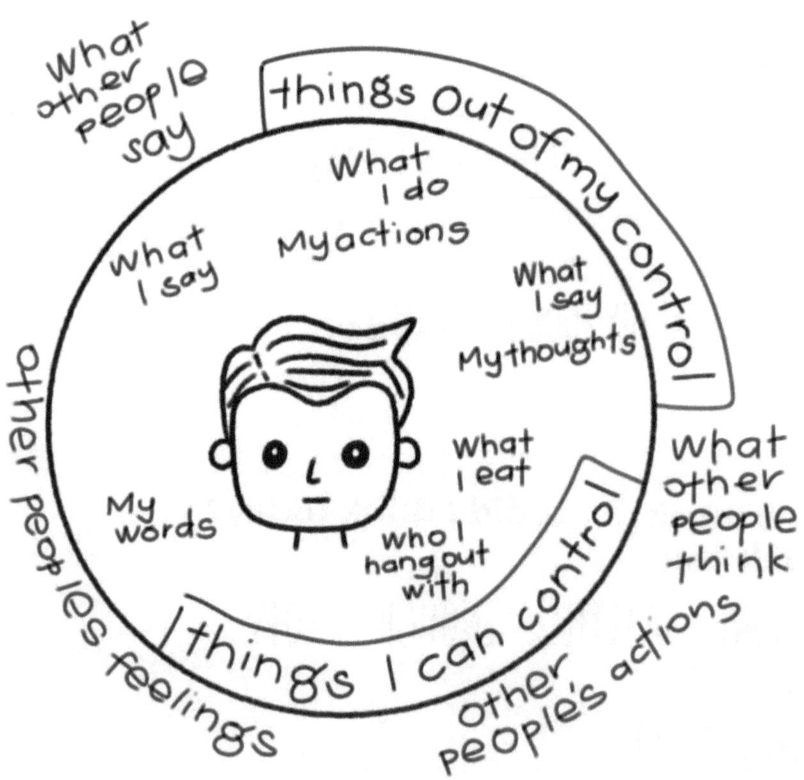

What other people say
things out of my control
What I do
My actions
What I say
What I say
My thoughts
other peoples feelings
What I eat
what other people think
My words
who I hang out with
things I can control
other people's actions

DATE: ___________________________

Something KIND I did today:

____

Today I am GRATEFUL for:
1.
2.
3.
4.

My FEELINGS and EMOTIONS today

MORNING   AFTERNOON   EVENING

Something that made me SMILE today:

____

Challenge tonight: Go outside when It's dark, and hopefully you will get to see the stars and gaze at the moon.

DAY 39   DATE: __________________________

EXERCISE **I did today:** __________________________ 

 NUTRITIOUS FOOD **I ate today:**

 UNHEALTHY FOOD **I ate today:**

How much WATER **did I drink today?**
Circle one

NONE   A LITTLE   ENOUGH   LOTS

Today I FELT:

____
____

HIGHLIGHT OF MY DAY TODAY:

____
____

 DATE: _______________________

EVALUATE

The BEST thing that happened this week:

____

____

The WORST thing that happened this week:

____

____

What could I do NEXT TIME to make it different/better?

____

____

What did I do that was the most KIND this week?

____

____

What was I CURIOUS about this week?

____

____

What did I CREATE this week?

____

____

Save/Spend/Share

How much money do I have? Am I saving for something? How much does it cost?

What could I do this week to earn some extra pocket money?

What am I planning to focus on or ACHIEVE for this next week ahead?

DATE: ______________________

Something KIND I did today:

____

Today I am GRATEFUL for:
1.
2.
3.
4.

My FEELINGS and EMOTIONS today

MORNING   AFTERNOON   EVENING

Something that made me SMILE today:

____

Limit your SCREEN TIME to become a happier you!

 DATE: _______________________

EXERCISE **I did today:** _______________________

NUTRITIOUS FOOD **I ate today:**

UNHEALTHY FOOD **I ate today:**

How much WATER **did I drink today?**
Circle one

NONE   A LITTLE   ENOUGH   LOTS

Today I FELT:

____

____

HIGHLIGHT OF MY DAY TODAY:

____

____

Routines I can do
that help me get
ready and tired for a
good nights sleep:

    DATE: _______________________

Something KIND I did today:

____

Today I am GRATEFUL for:
1.
2.
3.
4.

My FEELINGS and EMOTIONS today

MORNING   AFTERNOON   EVENING

Something that made me SMILE today:

____

2 things
I wish for:
1
2

 DATE: _______________________

EXERCISE **I did today:** _______________________

NUTRITIOUS FOOD **I ate today:**

UNHEALTHY FOOD **I ate today:**

How much WATER **did I drink today?**
Circle one

NONE   A LITTLE   ENOUGH   LOTS

Today I FELT:

____

____

HIGHLIGHT OF MY DAY TODAY:

____

____

The things I can do to calm myself down if I feel angry or frustrated:

Learn and practice healthy ways to cope when you feel angry, frustrated or stressed.

    DATE: _______________________

Something KIND I **did today:**

____

Today I am GRATEFUL **for:**
 1.
 2.
 3.
 4.

My FEELINGS **and** EMOTIONS **today**

MORNING   AFTERNOON   EVENING

Something that made me SMILE **today:**

____

Laugh lots

Dream Big

Give Love

Be Grateful

Have fun

And be Silly!

 DATE: _______________________

EXERCISE **I did today:** _______________________

NUTRITIOUS FOOD **I ate today:**

UNHEALTHY FOOD **I ate today:**

How much WATER **did I drink today?**
Circle one

NONE   A LITTLE   ENOUGH   LOTS

Today I FELT:

____

____

HIGHLIGHT OF MY DAY TODAY:

____

____

DATE: _______________________

Something KIND I did today:

____

Today I am GRATEFUL for:
1.
2.
3.
4.

My FEELINGS and EMOTIONS today

MORNING   AFTERNOON   EVENING

Something that made me SMILE today:

____

SAY THESE AFFIRMATIONS IN THE MIRROR TO MAKE YOU FEEL GREAT AND BELIEVE IN YOURSELF!

I am loved

I can be a great leader

I am happy

I have many friends

I respect myself

I can make a difference

I believe in myself

I am smart

I learn from my mistakes

I am important

I am safe and secure

I am AMAZING!

EVALUATE

The BEST thing that happened this week:

____

____

The WORST thing that happened this week:

____

____

What could I do NEXT TIME to make it different/better?

____

____

What did I do that was the most KIND this week?

____

____

What was I CURIOUS about this week?

____

____

What did I CREATE this week?

____

____

SAVE/SPEND/SHARE

How much money do I have? Am I saving for something? How much does it cost?

____

____

____

What could I do this week to earn some extra pocket money?

____

____

____

What am I planning to focus on or ACHIEVE for this next week ahead?

____

____

____

DAY 49

DATE: _______________________

EXERCISE **I did today:** _______________________ 

NUTRITIOUS FOOD **I ate today:**

UNHEALTHY FOOD **I ate today:**

How much WATER **did I drink today?**
Circle one

NONE   A LITTLE   ENOUGH   LOTS

Today I FELT:

____
____

HIGHLIGHT OF MY DAY TODAY:

____
____

DATE: _______________________

Something KIND I did today:

____

Today I am GRATEFUL for:
1.
2.
3.
4.

My FEELINGS and EMOTIONS today

MORNING   AFTERNOON   EVENING

Something that made me SMILE today:

____

FAVORITE PEOPLE I KNOW:

DAY 51   DATE: _______________________

EXERCISE **I did today:** _______________________

NUTRITIOUS FOOD **I ate today:**

UNHEALTHY FOOD **I ate today:**

How much WATER **did I drink today?**
Circle one

NONE   A LITTLE   ENOUGH   LOTS

Today I FELT:

____

____

HIGHLIGHT OF MY DAY TODAY:

____

____

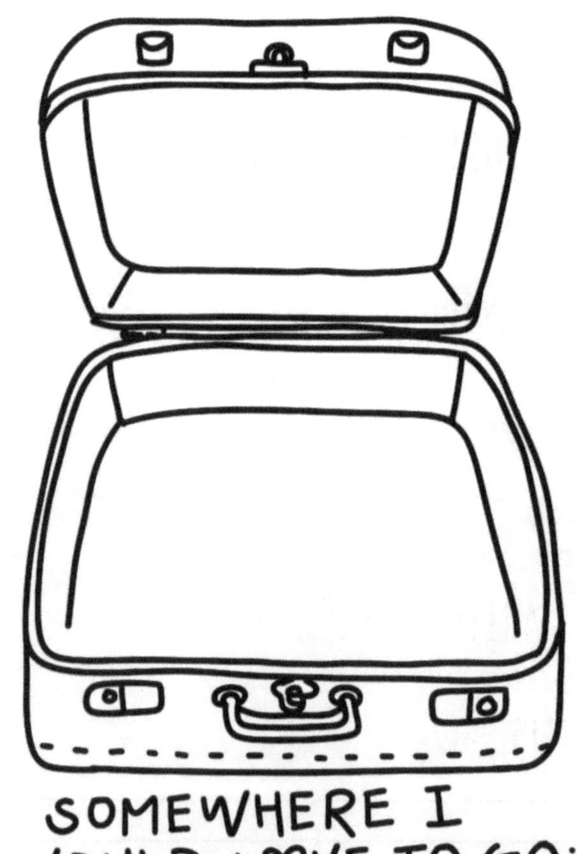

SOMEWHERE I
WOULD LOVE TO GO:

DATE: ________________________

Something KIND I did today:

____

Today I am GRATEFUL for:
1.
2.
3.
4.

My FEELINGS and EMOTIONS today

MORNING   AFTERNOON   EVENING

Something that made me SMILE today:

____

**Never compare myself
to others – as I am unique!**

Treat myself with kindness
and compassion especially
when life gets hard.

Talk to myself like I am my
own Best FRIEND!

DAY 53 DATE: _______________________

EXERCISE **I did today:** _______________________ 

NUTRITIOUS FOOD **I ate today:**

UNHEALTHY FOOD **I ate today:**

How much WATER **did I drink today?**
Circle one

NONE   A LITTLE   ENOUGH   LOTS

Today I FELT:

____

____

HIGHLIGHT OF MY DAY today:

____

____

be kind
be brave
be bold
be you!

   DATE: _______________________

Something KIND I **did today:**

____

Today I am GRATEFUL **for:**
  1.
  2.
  3.
  4.

My FEELINGS **and** EMOTIONS **today**

MORNING   AFTERNOON   EVENING

Something that made me SMILE **today:**

____

3 adults I can trust and that I can ask for help when I need it:

1.

2.

3.

<table><tr><td>DAY 55</td><td>DATE: _______________________</td></tr></table>

EXERCISE **I did today:** _______________________

NUTRITIOUS FOOD **I ate today:**

UNHEALTHY FOOD **I ate today:**

How much WATER **did I drink today?**
Circle one

NONE   A LITTLE   ENOUGH   LOTS

Today I FELT:

____

____

HIGHLIGHT OF MY DAY TODAY:

____

____

 DATE: _______________________

EVALUATE

The BEST thing that happened this week:
____
____

The WORST thing that happened this week:
____
____

What could I do NEXT TIME to make it different/better?
____
____

What did I do that was the most KIND this week?
____
____

What was I CURIOUS about this week?
____
____

What did I CREATE this week?
____
____

SAVE/SPEND/SHARE

How much money do I have? Am I saving for something? How much does it cost?

____

____

____

What could I do this week to earn some extra pocket money?

____

____

____

What am I planning to focus on or ACHIEVE for this next week ahead?

____

____

____

   DATE: _______________________

Something KIND I did today:

____

Today I am GRATEFUL for:
1.
2.
3.
4.

My FEELINGS and EMOTIONS today

MORNING   AFTERNOON   EVENING

Something that made me SMILE today:

____

I CAN HELP OTHER'S BY:

 DATE: _______________________

EXERCISE **I did today:** _______________________

NUTRITIOUS FOOD **I ate today:**

UNHEALTHY FOOD **I ate today:**

How much WATER **did I drink today?**
Circle one

NONE   A LITTLE   ENOUGH   LOTS

Today I FELT:

____
____

HIGHLIGHT OF MY DAY TODAY:

____
____

The more that
you READ,
The more
things you will
KNOW,
The more that
you will KNOW,
The more
places you'll
GO.

Dr Seuss

DATE: ______________________________

Something KIND I did today:

____

Today I am GRATEFUL for:
1.
2.
3.
4.

My FEELINGS and EMOTIONS today

MORNING   AFTERNOON   EVENING

Something that made me SMILE today:

____

  DATE: _______________________

EXERCISE **I did today:** _______________________

NUTRITIOUS FOOD **I ate today:**

UNHEALTHY FOOD **I ate today:**

How much WATER **did I drink today?**
Circle one

NONE   A LITTLE   ENOUGH   LOTS

Today I FELT:

____
____

HIGHLIGHT OF MY DAY TODAY:

____
____

Things I can do to cheer myself up, when I am feeling sad:

DAY 61 DATE: ___________________________

Something KIND I did today:

____

Today I am GRATEFUL for:
   1.
   2.
   3.
   4.

My FEELINGS and EMOTIONS today

MORNING   AFTERNOON   EVENING

Something that made me SMILE today:

____

Something I would never change about MYSELF:

    DATE: _______________________

EXERCISE **I did today:** _____________________ 

NUTRITIOUS FOOD **I ate today:**

UNHEALTHY FOOD **I ate today:**

How much WATER **did I drink today?**
Circle one
   NONE   A LITTLE   ENOUGH   LOTS

Today I FELT:
____
____

HIGHLIGHT OF MY DAY TODAY:
____
____

In a world

where you can choose

To be anything,

Choose to be

KIND

   DATE: _______________________

Something KIND **I did today:**

____

Today I am GRATEFUL **for:**
1.
2.
3.
4.

My FEELINGS **and** EMOTIONS **today**

MORNING   AFTERNOON   EVENING

Something that made me SMILE **today:**

____

Someone **I** look up to and ADMIRE:

   DATE: _______________________

EVALUATE

The BEST thing that happened this week:

____

____

The WORST thing that happened this week:

____

____

What could I do NEXT TIME to make it different/better?

____

____

What did I do that was the most KIND this week?

____

____

What was I CURIOUS about this week?

____

____

What did I CREATE this week?

____

____

Save/Spend/Share

How much money do I have? Am I saving for something? How much does it cost?

____

____

____

What could I do this week to earn some extra pocket money?

____

____

____

What am I planning to focus on or ACHIEVE for this next week ahead?

____

____

____

 DATE: ______________________

EXERCISE I did today: ______________________ 

NUTRITIOUS FOOD **I ate today:**

UNHEALTHY FOOD **I ate today:**

How much WATER **did I drink today?**
Circle one

NONE   A LITTLE   ENOUGH   LOTS

Today I FELT:

____
____

HIGHLIGHT OF MY DAY TODAY:

____
____

    DATE: _______________________

Something KIND I **did today:**

____

Today I am GRATEFUL **for:**
1.
2.
3.
4.

My FEELINGS **and** EMOTIONS **today**

MORNING   AFTERNOON   EVENING

Something that made me SMILE **today:**

____

You're BRAVER than you believe, STRONGER than you seem and SMARTER than you think.

A.A.Milne

 DATE: _______________________

EXERCISE **I did today:** _______________________

NUTRITIOUS FOOD **I ate today:**

UNHEALTHY FOOD **I ate today:**

How much WATER **did I drink today?**
Circle one

NONE   A LITTLE   ENOUGH   LOTS

Today I FELT:

____
____

HIGHLIGHT OF MY DAY TODAY:

____
____

I am
AMAZING
because:

DAY 68   DATE: _______________________

Something KIND I did today:

____

Today I am GRATEFUL for:
1.
2.
3.
4.

My FEELINGS and EMOTIONS today

MORNING   AFTERNOON   EVENING

Something that made me SMILE today:

____

If someone is mean to me
or bullies ME. The
Actions I can take are:

DAY 69 **DATE:** ___________________________

EXERCISE **I did today:** ___________________________ 

 **I ate today:**

 **I ate today:**

How much WATER **did I drink today?**
Circle one

NONE   A LITTLE   ENOUGH   LOTS

Today I FELT:

____

____

HIGHLIGHT OF MY DAY TODAY:

____

____

I am super **THANKFUL** for:

      DATE: _______________________

Something KIND I did today:

____

Today I am GRATEFUL for:
1.
2.
3.
4.

My FEELINGS and EMOTIONS today

MORNING   AFTERNOON   EVENING

Something that made me SMILE today:

____

A person who
never made a
mistake, never
tried anything
new.

Albert Einstein

 DATE: _______________________

EXERCISE **I did today:** ______________________ 

 NUTRITIOUS FOOD **I ate today:**

 UNHEALTHY FOOD **I ate today:**

How much WATER **did I drink today?**
Circle one

NONE   A LITTLE   ENOUGH   LOTS

Today I FELT:

____

____

HIGHLIGHT OF MY DAY TODAY:

____

____

 DATE: _______________________

EVALUATE

The BEST thing that happened this week:

____

____

The WORST thing that happened this week:

____

____

What could I do NEXT TIME to make it different/better?

____

____

What did I do that was the most KIND this week?

____

____

What was I CURIOUS about this week?

____

____

What did I CREATE this week?

____

____

Save/Spend/Share

How much money do I have? Am I saving for something? How much does it cost?

____

____

____

What could I do this week to earn some extra pocket money?

____

____

____

What am I planning to focus on or ACHIEVE for this next week ahead?

____

____

____

     DATE: _______________________

Something KIND I did today:

____

Today I am GRATEFUL for:
  1.
  2.
  3.
  4.

My FEELINGS and EMOTIONS today

MORNING   AFTERNOON   EVENING

Something that made me SMILE today:

____

Things
I love
to do on
Rainy and
Snowy
Days:

    DATE: _______________________

EXERCISE **I did today:** _____________________ 

NUTRITIOUS FOOD **I ate today:**

UNHEALTHY FOOD **I ate today:**

How much WATER **did I drink today?**
Circle one

NONE   A LITTLE   ENOUGH   LOTS

Today I FELT:

____

____

HIGHLIGHT OF MY DAY TODAY:

____

____

DON'T STOP UNTIL YOU'RE PROUD

  DATE: _______________________

Something KIND I **did today:**

____

Today I am GRATEFUL **for:**
1.
2.
3.
4.

My FEELINGS **and** EMOTIONS **today**

MORNING   AFTERNOON   EVENING

Something that made me SMILE **today:**

____

What makes a
GREAT FRIEND?

DAY 76 DATE: _______________________

EXERCISE **I did today:** _______________________

NUTRITIOUS FOOD **I ate today:**

UNHEALTHY FOOD **I ate today:**

How much WATER **did I drink today?**
Circle one

NONE   A LITTLE   ENOUGH   LOTS

Today I FELT:

____

____

HIGHLIGHT OF MY DAY TODAY:

____

____

                DATE: ________________________

Something KIND I did today:

____

Today I am GRATEFUL for:
    1.
    2.
    3.
    4.

My FEELINGS and EMOTIONS today

MORNING   AFTERNOON   EVENING

Something that made me SMILE today:

____

COURAGE
doesn't always ROAR
sometimes courage is
That little voice at
The end of the day that say's
"I will try again tomorrow."

Mary Radmacher

DAY 78   DATE: _______________________

EXERCISE I did today: _____________________ 

NUTRITIOUS FOOD **I ate today:**

UNHEALTHY FOOD **I ate today:**

How much WATER **did I drink today?
Circle one**

NONE   A LITTLE   ENOUGH   LOTS

Today I FELT:

____

____

HIGHLIGHT OF MY DAY TODAY:

____

____

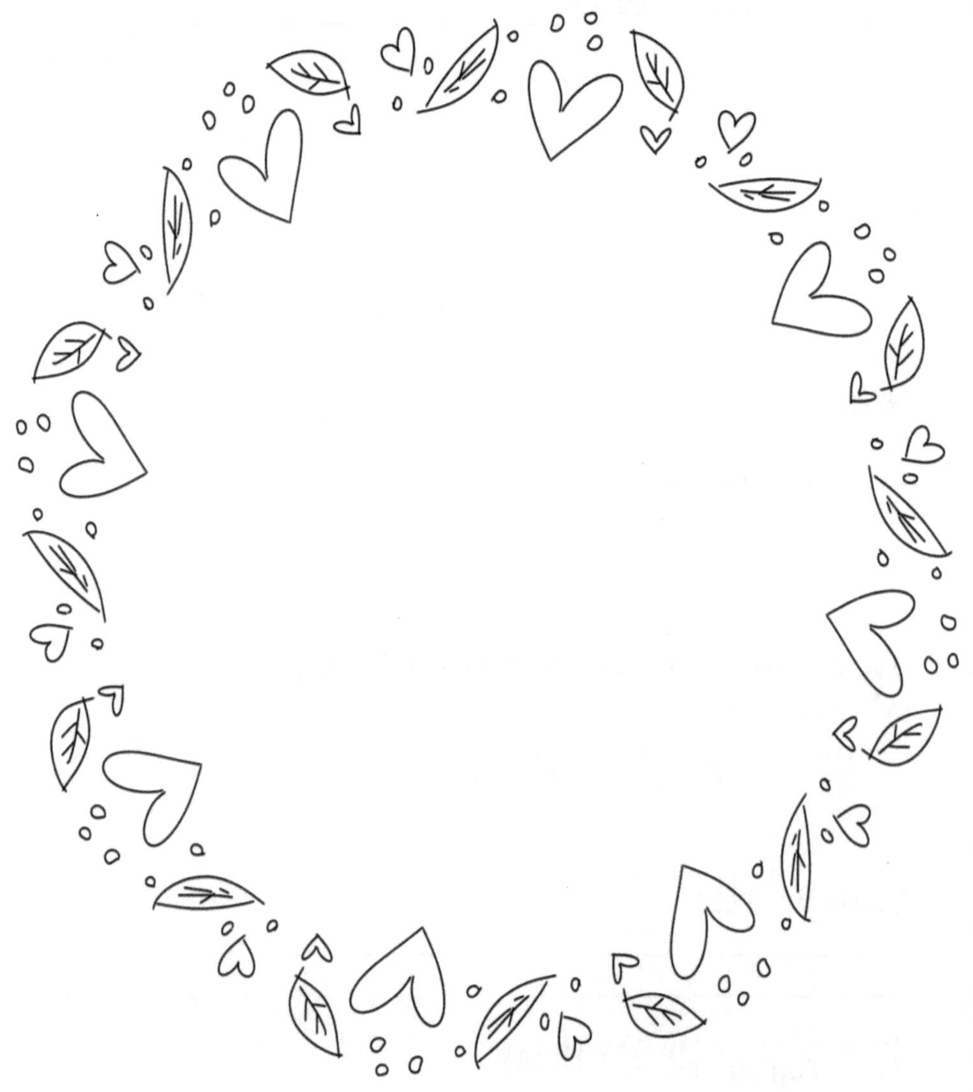

   DATE: _______________________

Something KIND I did today:

____

Today I am GRATEFUL for:
1.
2.
3.
4.

My FEELINGS and EMOTIONS today

MORNING   AFTERNOON   EVENING

Something that made me SMILE today:

____

Things I can do
To help support
Planet EARTH:

  DATE: _______________________

EVALUATE

The BEST **thing that happened this week:**

____

____

The WORST **thing that happened this week:**

____

____

What could I do NEXT TIME **to make it different/better?**

____

____

What did I do that was the most KIND **this week?**

____

____

What was I CURIOUS **about this week?**

____

____

What did I CREATE **this week?**

____

____

Save/Spend/Share

How much money do I have? Am I saving for something? How much does it cost?

____

____

____

What could I do this week to earn some extra pocket money?

____

____

____

What am I planning to focus on or ACHIEVE for this next week ahead?

____

____

____

  DATE: _______________________

EXERCISE **I did today:** _______________________

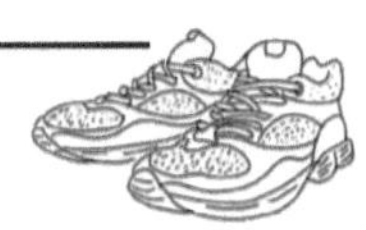

NUTRITIOUS FOOD **I ate today:**

UNHEALTHY FOOD **I ate today:**

How much WATER **did I drink today?**
Circle one

NONE   A LITTLE   ENOUGH   LOTS

Today I FELT:

____
____

HIGHLIGHT OF MY DAY TODAY:

____
____

     DATE: ______________________

Something KIND I did today:

____

Today I am GRATEFUL for:
  1.
  2.
  3.
  4.

My FEELINGS and EMOTIONS today

MORNING   AFTERNOON   EVENING

Something that made me SMILE today:

____

Be
CURIOUS
and
try new things!

     DATE: _______________________

EXERCISE **I did today:** _____________________

NUTRITIOUS FOOD **I ate today:**

UNHEALTHY FOOD **I ate today:**

How much WATER **did I drink today?**
Circle one

NONE   A LITTLE   ENOUGH   LOTS

Today I FELT:

____

____

HIGHLIGHT OF MY DAY TODAY:

____

____

Sometimes I feel sad and disappointed when:

To cheer myself up I:

DATE: _______________________

Something KIND **I did today:**

____

Today I am GRATEFUL **for:**
1.
2.
3.
4.

My FEELINGS **and** EMOTIONS **today**

MORNING   AFTERNOON   EVENING

Something that made me SMILE **today:**

____

Be a RAINBOW
in someone's
Cloud.

Maya Angelou

DAY 85   DATE: _______________________

EXERCISE **I did today:** _____________________

NUTRITIOUS FOOD **I ate today:**

UNHEALTHY FOOD **I ate today:**

How much WATER **did I drink today?**
Circle one

NONE   A LITTLE   ENOUGH   LOTS

Today I FELT:

____

____

HIGHLIGHT OF MY DAY TODAY:

____

____

 DATE: _______________________

Something KIND I did today:

____

Today I am GRATEFUL for:
1.
2.
3.
4.

My FEELINGS and EMOTIONS today

MORNING　　　AFTERNOON　　　EVENING

Something that made me SMILE today:

____

I am happy

I am brave

I am smart

I shine bright

I have happy thoughts

I am healthy and strong

I am kind

I try my best at all times

I manage my emotions

I am a great friend

I am LOVED

DAY 87   DATE: _______________________

EXERCISE **I did today:** _______________________

NUTRITIOUS FOOD **I ate today:**

UNHEALTHY FOOD **I ate today:**

How much WATER **did I drink today?**
Circle one

NONE   A LITTLE   ENOUGH   LOTS

Today I FELT:

____

____

HIGHLIGHT OF MY DAY TODAY:

____

____

 DATE: _______________________

EVALUATE

The BEST thing that happened this week:

____

____

The WORST thing that happened this week:

____

____

What could I do NEXT TIME to make it different/better?

____

____

What did I do that was the most KIND this week?

____

____

What was I CURIOUS about this week?

____

____

What did I CREATE this week?

____

____

Save/Spend/Share

How much money do I have? Am I saving for something? How much does it cost?

____

____

____

What could I do this week to earn some extra pocket money?

____

____

____

What am I planning to focus on or ACHIEVE for this next week ahead?

____

____

____

Certificate of ACHIEVEMENT

CONGRATULATIONS

____

FOR RECOGNITION OF
THE COMPLETION OF
MY JOURNAL

DATE: ___________________